CHATGPT UNLOCKED - A BEGINNERS GUIDE FOR PEOPLE 50+

First edition. September 22, 2024.

Copyright © 2024 Shane Lifeman.

ISBN: 979-8227080196

Written by Shane Lifeman.

Also by Shane Lifeman

Live Free Live Life
We are Jeff and Doris and We Survived Winning The Lottery
Starting Over With Nothings A Rags To Riches Strategy
My Life As A Millionaire Was To Much Work - Living Free Living Life Is Better
From Dream To Reality - A Step By Step Guide How To Move Abroad and Thrive

Standalone
The Power of One Content Repurposing Blueprint - Create Multiple Passive Income Streams
ChatGPT Unlocked - A Beginners Guide For People 50+

Watch for more at www.livefreelivelife.com.

Welcome To Our Introduction:

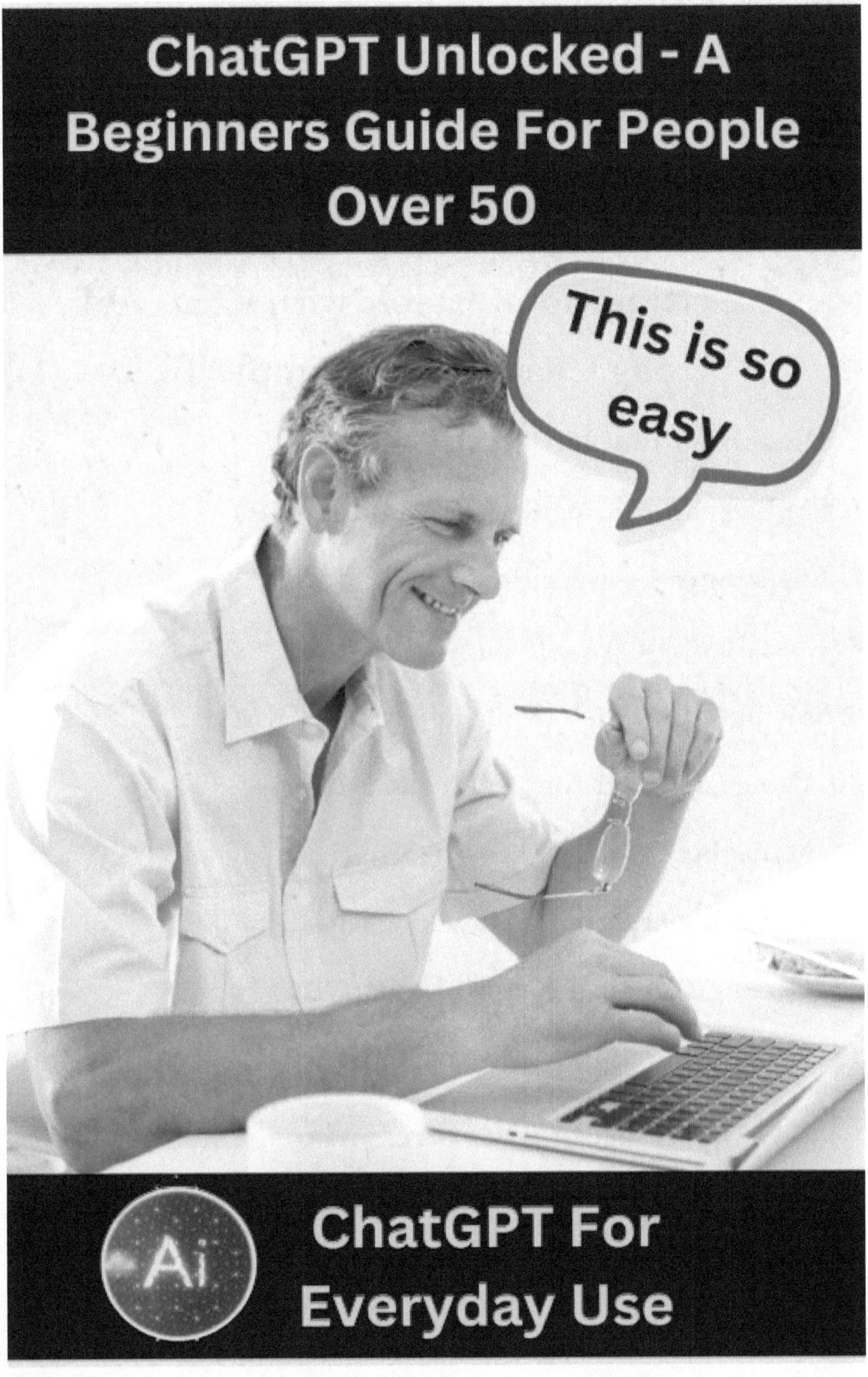

ChatGPT Unlocked - A Beginners Guide For People Over 50
This is so easy
Ai
ChatGPT For Everyday Use

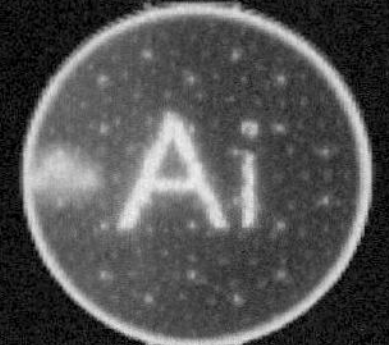

By: Shane Lifeman and Shalyn Publishing

Chapters:

Begin!

17. Conclusion: Your New Adventure with ChatGPT

Chapter 1:
Introduction to ChatGPT

In today's fast-paced, technology-driven world, having tools that can assist with everything from research to creative writing, and even answering general questions, can be a game-changer. One such tool is ChatGPT. But what exactly is ChatGPT, and how can it help in your day-to-day life? This chapter aims to give beginners an easy-to-understand overview of what ChatGPT is, how it works, and the ways it can assist you in accomplishing a variety of tasks.

What Is ChatGPT?

ChatGPT is an AI (Artificial Intelligence) language model developed by OpenAI. The "GPT" stands for "Generative Pre-trained Transformer," which means it is designed to generate human-like text based on input it receives. In simple terms, you type something (a question or a task), and ChatGPT responds with a well-thought-out answer, idea, or solution. It's just that easy to use.

ChatGPT's foundation is built on vast amounts of text data, meaning it has been trained using an immense range of information sources like books, websites, and articles. As a result, ChatGPT has acquired the ability to understand and generate text that is both coherent and contextually relevant. While it doesn't "think" or "understand" in the way humans do, it excels at identifying patterns in language and providing meaningful responses.

Key Features of ChatGPT

- **Text-based Interaction:** ChatGPT communicates purely through written text. You type in your queries, and it provides responses, making it incredibly easy to interact with.

- **Wide Range of Capabilities:** From answering factual questions to assisting with creative writing, brainstorming, and problem-solving, ChatGPT can assist in many different areas.

- **24/7 Availability:** Unlike human assistants, ChatGPT is always available whenever you need it, whether it's late at night or during busy working hours, ChatGPT is always ready and available, and caters to your schedule.

How Does ChatGPT Work?

To use ChatGPT, all you need is an internet connection and a platform that hosts the model, such as the OpenAI website, a specific app, or even integrations within other tools. Once you're ready, interacting with ChatGPT is as simple as typing in a question or task in the chat box

Here's a simplified breakdown of how ChatGPT works:

1. *Input Stage*: You provide a prompt, which can be a question, task, or instruction. For example, "What are some healthy dinner ideas?" or "Explain the solar system."

2. *Processing Stage*: ChatGPT processes the input using its deep learning model. This model breaks down your query, searches for patterns in its training data, and generates a response.

3. *Output Stage*: Within seconds, ChatGPT returns a response that matches your input. The more specific and clear your prompt, the better the response tends to be.

ChatGPT doesn't have real-time access to the internet, meaning it can't look up information on the spot. Instead, it relies on what it has learned during its training. Because of this, it's good at general information and creative tasks, but it may not always have the most up-to-date knowledge on rapidly changing topics like news or live sports.

Tips for Effective Interaction with ChatGPT

● Be Clear and Specific: The more detailed your question or task is, the better the response. Instead of "Tell me about history," try "Give me a brief overview of World War II." The More details you use in your query, the better the response will be

● Use Follow-Up Questions: You can continue a conversation with ChatGPT to refine your query or gather more details. For example, if you ask for dinner ideas, you can follow up with "Can you make that vegetarian?"

● Provide Context: If you're working on a specific project or task, giving context helps ChatGPT provide more relevant answers. For instance, "I'm working on a presentation for school. Can you help me explain how volcanoes work?"

How ChatGPT Can Assist with Daily Tasks

Now that you have an idea of what ChatGPT is and how it works, let's look at how it can help with everyday tasks.

1. General Information and Research

Need to find information on a topic but don't want to spend hours sifting through search results? ChatGPT can give you a concise, easy-to-understand explanation on a wide range of subjects. Whether it's learning about a historical event, understanding how a scientific process works, or getting quick facts, ChatGPT is like having a personal research assistant at your fingertips.

2. Writing Assistance

Struggling to find the right words for an email, essay, or blog post? ChatGPT can help by generating ideas, suggesting wording, or even writing entire drafts based on your input. You can use it to:

- Write business emails,
- Draft creative stories or blog posts,
- Generate ideas for social media captions or presentations.

3. Language Translation and Learning

Need help with a foreign language? ChatGPT can assist with basic translation tasks or provide you with explanations for different words, phrases, and grammar rules. It can even help you practice conversations in other languages.

4. Task Planning and Organization

From planning a vacation itinerary to organizing your daily to-do list, ChatGPT can help break down tasks into manageable steps. For instance, if you're planning a weekend getaway, you can ask ChatGPT to suggest places to visit, activities to do, and even generate packing lists.

5. Creative Brainstorming

Whether you're working on a project at work or a personal hobby, ChatGPT can be an excellent brainstorming partner. It can suggest ideas for stories, project names, product concepts, or even help generate solutions to problems you're facing.

6. Problem Solving

If you're stuck on a problem, whether it's related to work, school, or personal life, ChatGPT can offer possible

solutions. While it may not always have the "correct" answer, it can provide fresh perspectives or ideas that you might not have thought of before.

Conclusion

ChatGPT is an incredibly versatile tool that is easy to use for beginners. It offers assistance across a wide range of daily tasks—from research and writing to planning and problem-solving. Whether you need quick information, writing help, or just someone to bounce ideas off of, ChatGPT can be your go-to digital assistant.

By understanding how to interact with ChatGPT effectively, you can unlock its full potential and make your everyday tasks easier and more efficient. The key is to experiment, be clear with your queries, and enjoy the endless possibilities that this AI-powered tool has to offer!

Chapter 2:
Setting Up ChatGPT The Easy Way

Now that you have an understanding of what ChatGPT is and how it works, the next step is learning how to access and set it up on your devices. Whether you're using a computer, tablet, or smartphone, this chapter will walk you through, step by step, how to get started with ChatGPT. We'll cover different platforms where ChatGPT is available, and offer clear instructions for beginners. Don't worry—it's easier than you might think!

1. How to Access ChatGPT

Before diving into how to set up ChatGPT on different devices, let's first talk about where you can access it. ChatGPT is a cloud-based service, meaning you don't need to install any software. Instead, you interact with it through your web browser or dedicated apps.

Here are the most common ways to access ChatGPT:

- **OpenAI's Website:** This is the main platform to use ChatGPT directly from your browser.

- **Mobile Apps:** Some mobile apps integrate with ChatGPT, allowing you to interact with it on the go.

- **Third-Party Platforms:** Some websites and apps embed ChatGPT as part of their services for customer support, education, or productivity.

For now, let's focus on the most straightforward method—using OpenAI's website on various devices.

2. Accessing ChatGPT on a Computer (Windows/Mac)

If you're using a desktop or laptop computer, accessing ChatGPT is simple. Follow these steps:

Step 1: Open Your Web Browser

On your computer, open your preferred web browser. This could be Google Chrome, Firefox, Safari, or any other browser you use regularly. ChatGPT is compatible with most modern browsers.

Step 2: Visit OpenAI's Website

In the browser's address bar, type chat.openai.com and press Enter. This will take you to OpenAI's ChatGPT platform.

Step 3: Sign Up or Log In

● If this is your first time using ChatGPT, you'll need to sign up for an account. You can sign up using your email address, Google account, or even your Microsoft account. Simply click on "Sign up" and follow the on-screen instructions.

● If you already have an account, click Log in and enter your credentials.

Step 4: Start Using ChatGPT

Once you're logged in, you'll be brought to the ChatGPT interface. Here, you can type your questions or tasks into the input box at the bottom of the page and press Enter to submit them. ChatGPT will respond within seconds.

Tips for Computer Users:

● Bookmark the ChatGPT Page: You can bookmark the website for quick access in the future. In most browsers, just press Ctrl + D (Windows) or Cmd + D (Mac) to add it to your bookmarks.

● Keyboard Shortcuts: Use the Tab key to move through fields or press Enter to quickly send a query.

3. Accessing ChatGPT on a Tablet (iOS/Android)

If you prefer using a tablet, accessing ChatGPT is equally simple. Tablets like iPads or Android devices offer more flexibility with touchscreens while still giving you a larger display for reading ChatGPT's responses.

Step 1: Open Your Browser App

Open your tablet's internet browser app. On iOS devices, this could be Safari or Chrome, while Android users might use Chrome or Firefox.

Step 2: Visit OpenAI's Website

In the browser's address bar, type chat.openai.com and press Enter to access the ChatGPT platform.

Step 3: Sign Up or Log In

Just like on the computer, you'll need to either sign up or log in if you already have an account. The steps are the same as mentioned above.

Step 4: Start Interacting with ChatGPT

Once logged in, you'll see the familiar ChatGPT interface. You can use the tablet's on-screen keyboard to type your questions or tasks and press Send to interact with the AI.

Tips for Tablet Users:

- **Landscape Mode:** If you find the on-screen keyboard taking up too much space, rotate your tablet into landscape mode for a wider display.

- **Mobile Browser View:** Some mobile browsers offer a "desktop view" option if you want the page to look more like it does on a computer.

4. Accessing ChatGPT on a Smartphone (iOS/Android)

ChatGPT is also available on smartphones, making it easy to access while you're on the go. Whether you're using an iPhone or an Android device, here's how you can set it up:

Step 1: Open Your Mobile Browser

Just like with tablets, open the web browser app on your smartphone. This could be Safari for iPhones or Chrome for Android devices.

Step 2: Navigate to the OpenAI Website

In the address bar, type chat.openai.com and hit Go or Enter.

Step 3: Sign Up or Log In

On the mobile version of the site, you'll see a similar interface to the desktop version. You can sign up for an account or log in using your existing credentials.

Step 4: Start Typing Your Queries

Once logged in, you can immediately start using ChatGPT. Type your queries or instructions in the input box and press Send.

Tips for Smartphone Users:

- **Use Voice Typing:** Most modern smartphones allow you to use voice input. Instead of typing, you can speak your query into the microphone by tapping the voice typing button (often represented as a small microphone icon on the keyboard).

- **Pin ChatGPT to Your Home Screen:** Many mobile browsers, such as Safari and Chrome, let you add websites to your home screen as shortcuts. In Chrome, for example, tap the three dots in the top-right corner, then tap Add to Home screen. This will create an app-like icon for easy access.

- Use Mobile Apps: If you find the browser experience inconvenient, some third-party apps are integrated with ChatGPT and can be downloaded from the app store.

5. Accessing ChatGPT Through Other Platforms

Apart from using the web browser, ChatGPT can also be accessed through various third-party platforms or applications. These platforms often embed ChatGPT for different purposes, such as customer support or education. Some popular integrations include:

- Messaging Platforms: Some apps, like Slack or Telegram, may have ChatGPT bots integrated, allowing you to interact with the AI directly from your chat applications.

- Productivity Apps: Several productivity tools and apps may include ChatGPT to help with tasks like writing, summarizing, or brainstorming ideas.

- Custom Applications: Developers can integrate ChatGPT into their own software, creating customized experiences where ChatGPT assists in more specific tasks.

To access ChatGPT on any third-party platform, follow the instructions provided by the specific app or tool you're using.

6. Troubleshooting Common Issues

If you encounter any difficulties while setting up ChatGPT, don't worry—most problems are easily fixed. Here are some common issues and solutions:

Problem: "I Can't Log In to My Account"

- Solution: Double-check that you've entered the correct email and password. If you've forgotten your password, click on Forgot password to reset it via email.

Problem: "The Page Isn't Loading"

- **Solution:** Ensure you have a stable internet connection. Try refreshing the page or switching to a different browser if the issue persists.

Problem: "ChatGPT Isn't Responding to My Queries"

- **Solution:** This could be a temporary server issue. Wait for a few minutes and try again. If the problem continues, check the OpenAI status page to see if there are any ongoing issues.

Problem: "I'm Using a Mobile Browser, and the Text Box Is Hard to See"

- **Solution:** Try zooming in on the text box or switching to landscape mode for better visibility.

7. Keeping ChatGPT Updated

ChatGPT itself doesn't require you to install any updates since it's a cloud-based service. However, keeping your browser or third-party apps updated ensures that you have the best experience when using the tool.

Conclusion

Setting up ChatGPT on any device is a straightforward process that takes just a few minutes. Whether you're using a computer, tablet, or smartphone, the steps are simple and user-friendly. Once you're set up, you'll have access to a powerful tool that can assist with everything from research and writing to creative brainstorming and task management, all at your fingertips.

Chapter 3:
Getting Comfortable with ChatGPT

Now that you know how to set up and access ChatGPT, the next step is getting comfortable with how to interact with it. In this chapter, we will guide you through the best ways to ask questions, give commands, and understand the responses you receive from ChatGPT. As a beginner, you don't need to worry about using complicated language or jargon—ChatGPT is designed to respond to clear and simple instructions. With a few tips, you'll be able to get the most out of your interactions with this AI tool.

Understanding the Basics of Interacting with ChatGPT

When you communicate with ChatGPT, think of it as having a conversation with a helpful assistant. Just like talking to a person, you can ask questions or give commands, and ChatGPT will do its best to respond accurately and clearly. However, since ChatGPT is a language model, it doesn't have emotions or personal experiences—it's purely focused on providing answers based on the information it has been trained on.

Key Types of Interactions:

1. **Asking Questions:** You can ask ChatGPT to explain concepts, provide information, or answer factual questions.

○ Example: "What is photosynthesis?"

2. **Giving Commands:** You can ask ChatGPT to perform tasks like summarizing text, helping you draft an email, or brainstorming ideas.

○ Example: "Write a summary of the novel *To Kill a Mockingbird*."

3. **Having Conversations:** You can engage in longer, back-and-forth conversations, asking follow-up questions or refining your request as needed.

○ Example: "Can you give me more details about how plants produce oxygen during photosynthesis?"

Now, let's look at how to maximize your interactions by asking clear questions, giving useful commands, and understanding ChatGPT's responses.

Asking Good Questions

One of the simplest ways to interact with ChatGPT is by asking questions. The AI can respond to a wide variety of queries, but how you ask your question can affect the quality of the response. Here are some tips to help you ask better questions:

1. Be Clear and Specific

The more specific your question is, the more accurate and useful ChatGPT's response will be. If you ask a vague question, you might get a broad or less helpful answer.

- Vague: "Tell me about history."
- Specific: "Can you explain the causes of World War I?"

Being specific helps ChatGPT focus on the information that's most relevant to your query.

2. Ask One Question at a Time

If you ask multiple questions in one sentence, the response might get confusing or incomplete. It's better to break your questions into smaller, separate prompts.

- Less effective: "What are the best novels ever written, and can you summarize one for me?"

- More effective: "What are some of the best novels ever written?" followed by, "Can you summarize *Pride and Prejudice* for me?"

3. Use Follow-Up Questions

ChatGPT can remember the context of your conversation, so feel free to ask follow-up questions to dive deeper into a topic. For example, after asking ChatGPT for an explanation of a historical event, you might ask for more specific details.

- Initial Question: "What is the Great Depression?"

- Follow-Up: "What caused the stock market crash that started the Great Depression?"

This allows you to gather more information step by step.

Giving Commands Effectively

Aside from asking questions, ChatGPT can follow commands to perform tasks like generating ideas, creating lists, or helping with writing. To get the best results from these interactions, it's helpful to give clear and concise instructions.

1. Be Direct and to the Point

When giving a command, keep it short and straightforward. This helps ChatGPT understand exactly what you want it to do.

- Less effective: "Can you maybe sort of help me write something that explains photosynthesis?"

- More effective: "Write a brief explanation of photosynthesis."

2. Provide Context When Needed

If your command involves a specific task like writing or brainstorming, it's often helpful to provide some context or details. This helps ChatGPT tailor its response to your needs.

- Basic Command: "Write a product description."

- Command with Context: "Write a product description for a new eco-friendly water bottle that keeps drinks cold for 24 hours."

The more information you give, the better ChatGPT can complete the task.

3. Experiment with Different Commands

ChatGPT is versatile, so don't hesitate to experiment with various commands. You can ask it to write stories, generate ideas, answer technical questions, or even give you step-by-step instructions for tasks. The more you try, the better you'll understand how ChatGPT responds to different types of requests.

- Brainstorming: "Give me five creative ideas for a birthday party."
- Writing Help: "Write a professional email asking for a meeting."
- Learning Aid: "Explain how the water cycle works."

Understanding ChatGPT's Responses

After you ask a question or give a command, ChatGPT will generate a response based on its training data. While ChatGPT tries to provide accurate and useful answers, there are some things to keep in mind when interpreting its responses.

1. ChatGPT Isn't Perfect

ChatGPT can make mistakes or provide outdated information, especially if the topic is something that changes frequently, like recent news or scientific discoveries. It's always a good idea to double-check the facts, especially for important matters.

- Example: "What is the capital of Australia?"

  o ChatGPT will likely give you the correct answer (Canberra), but for more complex or evolving topics, a quick fact-check is a good idea.

2. Rephrase Your Question If Necessary

If ChatGPT's response isn't quite what you expected, don't hesitate to rephrase your question or command. Sometimes, small changes in how you ask a question can lead to a much clearer or more accurate answer.

● Original: "Explain physics."

● Rephrased: "Can you explain the basic principles of Newton's laws of motion?"

3. Ask for Clarification

If a response seems too complex or you don't fully understand it, you can always ask ChatGPT to simplify or clarify its answer. This is especially helpful if you're dealing with technical or detailed topics.

● Clarification Request: "Can you explain that in simpler terms?"

ChatGPT is designed to be flexible, so it can adjust its explanations to better suit your level of understanding.

4. Conversational Tone

ChatGPT's responses are conversational, meaning it tries to communicate in a natural and human-like manner. This makes it easier for beginners to interact without feeling overwhelmed by overly formal or technical language.

● Friendly Interaction: "What's the weather like today in New York?"

○ Response: "I don't have live weather data, but you can check an app like Weather.com for the latest updates."

Conclusion

Getting comfortable with ChatGPT is all about practicing how to ask questions and give commands effectively. The more you interact with the AI, the better you'll get at receiving the kind of information or help you're looking for. Remember to be clear, specific, and patient as you explore all the different ways ChatGPT can assist you. Whether you're asking simple questions or giving more complex commands, this AI tool is here to make your tasks easier and your learning experience smoother!

Chapter 4:
Using ChatGPT for Simple Tasks

Now that you're more comfortable interacting with ChatGPT, let's explore how it can help you with everyday tasks. While ChatGPT isn't exactly a virtual assistant like Siri or Google Assistant (it can't set alarms or reminders directly), it can still simplify your life by helping with planning, organizing, and finding information. In this chapter, we'll cover practical ways to use ChatGPT for simple tasks, such as creating shopping lists, setting reminders (indirectly), and finding information online.

1. Creating Shopping Lists

One of the most common everyday tasks is writing a shopping list. ChatGPT can help you generate lists quickly based on your needs. Whether it's for groceries, home supplies, or specific events, ChatGPT can assist in organizing your items efficiently.

Example of Creating a Grocery List:

Let's say you need to create a grocery list for the week, but you aren't sure where to start. You can ask ChatGPT to help:

- You: "Help me create a grocery list for a week's worth of meals."

- ChatGPT: "Sure! What kind of meals are you planning? Do you need breakfast, lunch, and dinner items?"

After providing some details about your meal plans or dietary preferences, ChatGPT can give you a complete list of groceries to buy. Here's a more detailed interaction:

- You: "I'm planning to make spaghetti, chicken salad, and pancakes for dinner this week. Can you help me make a grocery list?"

- ChatGPT: "Of course! Here's a basic grocery list based on your meals:

○ Spaghetti Ingredients: Spaghetti pasta, ground beef, tomato sauce, garlic, onions, olive oil, Parmesan cheese.

○ Chicken Salad Ingredients: Chicken breasts, lettuce, cherry tomatoes, cucumbers, olive oil, balsamic vinegar.

○ Pancakes Ingredients: Pancake mix, eggs, milk, maple syrup, butter.

○ You may also want to add essentials like snacks, drinks, and any other items you regularly use!"

Tailoring the List to Your Preferences:

You can also ask ChatGPT to customize the list based on specific diets or preferences:

● You: "Can you make that list vegetarian?"

● ChatGPT: "Sure! Here's a vegetarian version:

○ Spaghetti Ingredients: Spaghetti pasta, marinara sauce, garlic, onions, olive oil, Parmesan cheese.

○ Salad Ingredients: Lettuce, cherry tomatoes, cucumbers, chickpeas, olive oil, balsamic vinegar.

○ Pancakes Ingredients: Pancake mix, eggs, milk, maple syrup, butter."

Managing Additional Categories:

If you want to organize your shopping list into categories for easier shopping, ChatGPT can help with that, too:

● You: "Can you group the list into categories like fruits, vegetables, and dairy?"

● ChatGPT: "Certainly! Here's the list organized:

○ Vegetables: Garlic, onions, lettuce, cherry tomatoes, cucumbers.

○ Grains: Spaghetti pasta, pancake mix.

○ Dairy: Parmesan cheese, eggs, milk, butter.

○ Other: Olive oil, balsamic vinegar, marinara sauce, maple syrup."

By asking ChatGPT to break things down, you can make your shopping experience much more manageable.

2. Setting Reminders (Indirectly)

While ChatGPT can't directly set reminders for you like some other voice assistants, it can still assist in the process by helping you plan out what you need to do and when to do it. You can use ChatGPT to create a list of reminders and then manually input them into your phone, calendar app, or reminder tool.

Example of Creating a Reminder List:

Imagine you have a busy week ahead and want to keep track of things to do each day. You can ask ChatGPT for help:

● You: "Can you help me plan my week? I have a meeting on Wednesday, a doctor's appointment on Thursday, and a friend's birthday on Friday."

● ChatGPT: "Here's a plan for your week:

○ Monday: Catch up on emails, prepare for Wednesday's meeting.

○ Tuesday: Finalize presentation for Wednesday's meeting.

○ Wednesday: Attend a meeting at [insert time].

○ Thursday: Doctor's appointment at [insert time]. Make sure to bring any necessary documents.

○ Friday: Buy a gift for your friend's birthday. Celebrate in the evening!"

Planning Daily Tasks:

You can also ask ChatGPT for suggestions on managing your daily to-do lists:

- You: "I need help organizing my tasks for tomorrow."

- ChatGPT: "Sure! What tasks do you need to get done?"

- You: "I need to finish a work report, go to the grocery store, and call my bank."

- ChatGPT: "Here's a simple plan for your day:

○ Morning: Finish the work report by 11 AM.

○ Afternoon: Go to the grocery store after lunch.

○ Evening: Call your bank before they close at 5 PM."

Once ChatGPT helps you create this plan, you can manually enter these reminders into your phone or calendar.

Using ChatGPT to Prioritize Tasks:

If you're unsure which tasks to tackle first, ChatGPT can help you prioritize:

- You: "I have too many things to do tomorrow. How should I prioritize these tasks?"

- ChatGPT: "Let's prioritize based on urgency and time:

○ Top Priority: Finish the work report (since it's likely tied to a deadline).

○ Medium Priority: Call your bank (important but can be done anytime before closing).

○ Low Priority: Grocery shopping (this can be done later in the day when you have more time)."

This structured approach can make your day more manageable.

3. Finding Information Online

ChatGPT excels at helping you find general information, saving you time from scouring the web yourself. While it doesn't have live access to the internet (meaning it can't look up the latest news or real-time data), it's trained on a large amount of information and can answer a wide range of questions.

Example of Looking Up General Information:

Let's say you want to know more about a specific topic, like a historical event or a scientific concept:

- You: "What is the theory of evolution?"

- ChatGPT: "The theory of evolution, proposed by Charles Darwin, explains how species of living organisms change over time through a process called natural selection. In this process, individuals with traits that are better suited to their environment are more likely to survive and reproduce, passing those traits on to the next generation. Over many generations, this can lead to significant changes in species."

ChatGPT can give you quick and simple explanations on a variety of topics, from science and history to entertainment and pop culture.

Getting Help with Research:

If you're working on a school project or need some basic research help, ChatGPT can be a great resource for gathering information:

● You: "I'm writing a paper on climate change. Can you give me a brief summary?"

● ChatGPT: "Climate change refers to long-term shifts in weather patterns and global temperatures, primarily due to human activities like burning fossil fuels, deforestation, and industrial processes. These activities release greenhouse gasses like carbon dioxide and methane into the atmosphere, trapping heat and causing global warming. The effects of climate change include rising sea levels, more extreme weather events, and damage to ecosystems."

While ChatGPT can't cite sources for you, it can help you understand basic concepts and point you in the right direction for deeper research.

Getting Quick Definitions and Explanations:

If you're not sure about the meaning of a word or a concept, you can ask ChatGPT for a quick definition or explanation:

● You: "What does 'photosynthesis' mean?"

● ChatGPT: "Photosynthesis is the process by which plants, algae, and some bacteria convert sunlight into chemical energy. During photosynthesis, plants use sunlight, water, and carbon dioxide to produce oxygen and glucose, which they use as food."

This saves you from having to search through multiple websites for a clear, concise answer.

4. Using ChatGPT for Brainstorming

ChatGPT can also help with brainstorming ideas, whether it's for personal projects, work, or hobbies. If you need help coming up with ideas, you can ask ChatGPT for suggestions:

Example of Brainstorming for Personal Projects:

- You: "I want to start a new hobby, but I'm not sure what to do. Can you suggest some hobbies?"

- ChatGPT: "Here are some ideas for new hobbies you might enjoy:

  ○ Painting or drawing,

  ○ Learning a musical instrument,

  ○ Photography,

  ○ Gardening,

  ○ Cooking or baking,

  ○ Learning a new language."

Brainstorming for Work or School:

- You: "Can you help me brainstorm some ideas for a marketing campaign?"

- ChatGPT: "Certainly! Here are some ideas for a marketing campaign:

  ○ Host a giveaway on social media to engage with customers.

  ○ Create a referral program where current customers can earn rewards for bringing in new customers.

  ○ Collaborate with influencers or bloggers in your industry to reach a larger audience."

Whether you're looking for creative inspiration or solutions to problems, ChatGPT is a helpful tool for brainstorming.

Chapter 5:
Organizing Your Life with ChatGPT

In today's fast-paced world, staying organized can be challenging. Fortunately, ChatGPT can assist in planning your day, managing events, and keeping track of to-do lists seamlessly. Below, we explore ten practical examples of how you can leverage ChatGPT to make your daily life more organized.

1. Daily Schedule Planning

ChatGPT can help you create a detailed daily schedule based on your priorities and deadlines. Simply provide your list of tasks, and it will suggest an optimized timeline, breaking down your day into manageable chunks.

Example:
"Here's your schedule for today:

- 9:00 AM - 10:00 AM: Team meeting
- 10:15 AM - 11:00 AM: Review project proposal
- 11:15 AM - 12:30 PM: Client follow-ups
- 1:00 PM - 2:00 PM: Lunch and personal time
- 2:00 PM - 3:30 PM: Work on report draft."

2. Setting and Managing Reminders

Forgetfulness can disrupt your plans. ChatGPT can set up reminders for key activities, meetings, or even simple tasks like taking medication. This ensures you don't miss any important commitments.

Example:
"I'll remind you at 2:00 PM to send the report to your manager."

3. Creating To-Do Lists

You can use ChatGPT to generate, organize, and prioritize your to-do lists. It can categorize tasks into urgent, high-priority, and low-priority, making it easier to tackle them efficiently.

Example:
"Today's to-do list:

1. Finalize presentation (High Priority)
2. Respond to client emails (Medium Priority)
3. Research new marketing strategies (Low Priority)."

4. Event Planning Assistance

Whether you're organizing a birthday party or a corporate event, ChatGPT can assist in planning every detail, from sending out invitations to scheduling the event agenda.

Example:
"For your birthday party, I suggest:

- 6:00 PM - 6:30 PM: Guests arrive and mingle

- 6:30 PM - 7:00 PM: Dinner
- 7:00 PM - 8:00 PM: Games and activities
- 8:00 PM: Cake cutting and speeches."

5. Meeting Coordination

Managing multiple meetings can be tricky. ChatGPT can schedule meetings, send out invites, and even create agendas for discussions based on your input.

Example:

"Your meeting with the marketing team is scheduled for 11:00 AM tomorrow. Here's a suggested agenda:

1. Review campaign performance
2. Discuss upcoming promotions
3. Allocate budget for Q4."

6. Travel Itinerary Management

Planning a trip? ChatGPT can compile your travel details into a cohesive itinerary, including flight times, hotel bookings, and sightseeing plans.

Example:

"Your itinerary for the New York trip:

- 8:00 AM: Flight from LA to NYC
- 1:00 PM: Check-in at Hotel Central
- 2:30 PM: Lunch at Joe's Café
- 4:00 PM: Visit the Metropolitan Museum of Art."

7. Budget and Expense Tracking

Staying on top of finances is crucial. ChatGPT can help you create a budget, track your expenses, and provide suggestions for staying within your financial limits.

Example:

"This month's budget:

- Groceries: $400 (You've spent $320 so far)
- Entertainment: $150 (Remaining: $50)
- Utilities: $100 (You've paid $80)."

8. Project Management Support

For complex projects, ChatGPT can help break down tasks, set deadlines, and monitor progress. It can act as a virtual project manager, ensuring you're on track.

Example:
"Project Plan:

1. Phase 1 - Research (Deadline: Sept 30)
2. Phase 2 - Development (Deadline: Oct 15)
3. Phase 3 - Testing (Deadline: Oct 30)
    Current Status: Phase 1 completed on time."

9. Personal Goal Tracking

Whether it's fitness, learning a new skill, or reading more books, ChatGPT can help you set personal goals and track your progress with regular updates and motivation.

Example:
"Fitness Goal Update:

- Week 1: Ran 5 miles
- Week 2: Ran 6 miles
- Goal: 7 miles by next week."

10. Automating Routine Tasks

From sending emails to setting up automated messages, ChatGPT can streamline repetitive tasks, freeing up more time for you to focus on what truly matters.

Example:

"I've set up an email draft for your weekly status report. Would you like me to send it now?"

Conclusion

ChatGPT can be a powerful ally in staying organized, reducing stress, and enhancing productivity. Whether you need help with day-to-day scheduling or complex project management, these ten examples demonstrate the many ways you can integrate ChatGPT into your organizational toolkit. By harnessing the power of AI, you can ensure that nothing falls through the cracks and that every day is well-planned and productive

Chapter 6:

Finding and Sharing Recipes with ChatGPT

Cooking at home can be both rewarding and challenging, especially when you're short on time or inspiration. ChatGPT can be your personal culinary assistant, helping you discover new recipes, customize meal plans, and even create a full week's menu that fits your dietary needs. In this chapter, we'll explore how ChatGPT can simplify your cooking experience and keep your meals exciting and nutritious.

Discovering New Recipes

When you're looking for something new to cook, ChatGPT can provide a variety of recipe ideas based on your preferences or ingredients you already have. Whether you're craving Italian pasta or a quick stir-fry, just ask for recommendations, and you'll get detailed recipes in seconds.

Example:

"I have chicken, broccoli, and pasta. What can I make?"

Response: "How about a creamy chicken broccoli Alfredo? Here's a quick recipe: Cook the pasta, sauté chicken and broccoli with garlic, and then mix in cream and Parmesan cheese."

Customizing Meal Plans

Meal planning can be overwhelming, especially if you have dietary restrictions or specific goals like weight loss or muscle gain. ChatGPT can create customized meal plans that fit your needs, providing balanced and diverse meal options for breakfast, lunch, and dinner.

Example:

"I'm looking for a high-protein, low-carb meal plan for the week."

Response: "Here's a 3-day plan:

● Day 1: Breakfast: Greek yogurt with nuts. Lunch: Grilled chicken salad. Dinner: Baked salmon with asparagus.

● Day 2: Breakfast: Scrambled eggs with spinach. Lunch: Turkey lettuce wraps. Dinner: Beef stir-fry with broccoli.

● Day 3: Breakfast: Cottage cheese with berries. Lunch: Tuna salad. Dinner: Chicken zucchini boats."

Generating Weekly Meal Ideas

If you're tired of eating the same dishes, ChatGPT can generate a week's worth of varied and healthy meal ideas. This way, you don't have to spend time brainstorming each day, and you can ensure a balanced diet throughout the week.

Example:

"Can you suggest a week's worth of dinner ideas?"

Response:

- Monday: Spaghetti with turkey meatballs and marinara sauce.

- Tuesday: Grilled shrimp tacos with avocado salsa.

- Wednesday: Quinoa-stuffed bell peppers with black beans and cheese.

- Thursday: Baked chicken thighs with roasted sweet potatoes and green beans.

- Friday: Thai coconut curry with tofu and vegetables.

- Saturday: Homemade veggie pizza with a side salad.

- Sunday: Slow-cooked beef stew with carrots and potatoes.

Sharing Recipes with Friends

Found a recipe you love? ChatGPT can help format and share recipes with friends or family. You can request a neatly organized version of any recipe, complete with ingredients and step-by-step instructions, making it easy to send via text or email.

Example:

"Can you format this chicken curry recipe to share with my friend?"

Response:

"Chicken Curry Recipe:

Ingredients:

- 2 chicken breasts, diced
- 1 onion, chopped

- 2 garlic cloves, minced
- 1 cup coconut milk
- 2 tbsp curry powder

Instructions:

1. Sauté onion and garlic in oil until soft.
2. Add chicken and cook until browned.
3. Stir in curry powder and coconut milk. Simmer for 15 minutes. Serve with rice."

Conclusion

With ChatGPT as your kitchen companion, meal planning and recipe discovery are no longer daunting tasks. You can easily find new recipes, tailor meal plans to your lifestyle, and generate a week's worth of healthy meals. By making cooking more accessible and fun, ChatGPT helps you enjoy nutritious, home-cooked meals every day

Chapter 7:
Engaging in Conversations with AI

ChatGPT is more than just a tool for productivity; it can also be a companion for meaningful conversations and intellectual discussions. Whether you're looking to explore new ideas, seek advice, or simply chat, this AI can make interactions enjoyable and thought-provoking. In this chapter, we'll share tips on how to have friendly and engaging conversations with ChatGPT, making the most of its potential for companionship and mental stimulation.

Starting a Conversation

You can approach ChatGPT like you would a friendly acquaintance. Begin with a simple greeting or ask a question about a topic you're curious about. The more specific you are, the better the response will be.

Example:

"Hi, ChatGPT! I've been thinking about learning a new language. Do you have any tips?"

Response: "Hello! Learning a new language is a great goal. I recommend starting with a few basic phrases and practicing them daily. Apps like Duolingo or Memrise can also help you build vocabulary and grammar skills."

Exploring Interests and Hobbies

ChatGPT can engage in conversations about your interests and hobbies, from books and movies to sports and gardening. You can discuss your favorite topics, ask for recommendations, or share your own experiences.

Example:

"I'm a big fan of science fiction novels. Do you have any book recommendations?"

Response: "If you enjoy science fiction, you might like 'Dune' by Frank Herbert for its epic world-building, or 'The Three-Body Problem' by Liu Cixin, which offers a unique take on first contact with an alien civilization."

Seeking Advice and Support

While ChatGPT isn't a substitute for professional advice, it can offer general guidance or a listening ear. If you're feeling stuck on a decision or need help organizing your thoughts, ChatGPT can provide a different perspective or suggest practical steps.

Example:

"I've been feeling overwhelmed with work. How can I manage my time better?"

Response: "It's tough when work feels overwhelming. One approach is to prioritize your tasks using the Eisenhower Matrix—divide them into urgent/important, not urgent/important, urgent/not important, and not urgent/not important categories. This helps focus on what truly needs your attention."

Learning and Exploring New Topics

For intellectual stimulation, you can ask ChatGPT to explain complex topics in simple terms, explore philosophical questions, or discuss current events. It's like having a conversation with a well-read friend who's always willing to share knowledge.

Example:

"Can you explain what quantum computing is in a simple way?"

Response: "Sure! Quantum computing uses the principles of quantum mechanics to process information in a way that's fundamentally different from traditional computers. It leverages quantum bits, or qubits, which can represent both 0 and 1 simultaneously, allowing it to solve certain problems much faster."

Creating a Positive Tone

If you're looking for a friendly or uplifting chat, you can ask ChatGPT to share positive quotes, funny anecdotes, or even engage in light-hearted banter. It's a great way to brighten your day or take a break from more serious conversations.

Example:

"Tell me a fun fact or something interesting!"

Response: "Did you know that honey never spoils? Archaeologists have found pots of honey in ancient Egyptian tombs that are over 3,000 years old and still perfectly edible!"

Using ChatGPT for Creative Writing

If you're into creative writing or storytelling, ChatGPT can help brainstorm ideas, create characters, or even draft short stories and poems. It's a useful tool for overcoming writer's block or simply experimenting with new concepts.

Example:

"I'm thinking of writing a fantasy story. Can you help me come up with a plot?"

Response: "Absolutely! How about a story where a young healer discovers they have the power to communicate with the spirits of the forest? When an ancient evil threatens their village, they must team up with a misunderstood outcast to protect their home."

Conclusion

Engaging in conversations with ChatGPT can be both enjoyable and enriching. Whether you're seeking companionship, intellectual stimulation, or creative inspiration, the possibilities are endless. By approaching these interactions with curiosity and an open mind, you can make the most of your conversations with AI, adding a new dimension of dialogue and connection to your daily life.

Chapter 8:
ChatGPT as a Travel Planner

Planning a trip can be exciting but also overwhelming with all the details to consider. From deciding where to go and what to see, to finding the best activities and restaurants, organizing a memorable vacation requires time and effort. ChatGPT can make this process much smoother by acting as your personal travel planner. In this chapter, we'll explore how to use ChatGPT for generating travel ideas, planning itineraries, booking activities, and learning about new destinations—all in a way that's easy and efficient.

Getting Travel Inspiration

If you're not sure where to go on your next vacation, ChatGPT can provide travel inspiration based on your preferences, such as your favorite activities, climate preferences, or budget. You can ask for suggestions tailored to different seasons, cultural experiences, or even hidden gems off the beaten path.

Example:

"I'm looking for a unique destination for a spring getaway. Any ideas?"

Response: "How about visiting Kyoto, Japan, during cherry blossom season? You can enjoy beautiful temples, traditional tea ceremonies, and the famous Philosopher's Path lined with blooming sakura trees."

Creating Custom Itineraries

Once you've chosen a destination, ChatGPT can help you plan a detailed itinerary. Whether you're visiting a city for a weekend or exploring a country for two weeks, it can suggest daily activities, local attractions, and the best times to visit popular spots, making sure your trip is well-organized and fulfilling.

Example:

"I'm planning a 3-day trip to Paris. Can you suggest an itinerary?"

Response:

"Here's a suggested 3-day itinerary for Paris:

- Day 1: Start with a visit to the Louvre Museum in the morning. After lunch, stroll through the Tuileries Garden and end the day with a Seine River cruise.

- Day 2: Spend the day exploring the historic Montmartre neighborhood, visiting the Sacré-Cœur Basilica, and enjoying an evening at a local café.

- Day 3: Visit the Eiffel Tower in the morning. In the afternoon, explore the Latin Quarter and finish with dinner in a traditional French bistro."

Booking Activities and Accommodations

While ChatGPT cannot make reservations directly, it can guide you on how to find and book the best activities, tours, and accommodations. You can ask for recommendations on reliable booking platforms, read reviews, and compare options based on your preferences and budget.

Example:

"What are some good websites to book guided tours in Rome?"

Response: "For guided tours in Rome, you can check websites like Viator, GetYourGuide, or Airbnb Experiences. They offer a variety of tours from Colosseum skip-the-line tickets to food and wine tastings. Be sure to read reviews to find the best experience for you."

Learning About New Places

ChatGPT can provide you with interesting facts, cultural insights, and historical information about your chosen destination, enriching your travel experience. You can learn about local customs, must-try dishes, or the history behind famous landmarks, making your trip not just a visit but a deeper exploration.

Example:

"I'm traveling to Istanbul. Can you tell me more about its history?"

Response: "Istanbul is a city that spans two continents, Europe and Asia, and has a rich history as the capital of the Byzantine and Ottoman Empires. Key landmarks like Hagia Sophia, once a cathedral and later a mosque, reflect the city's diverse cultural heritage. Be sure to visit the Grand Bazaar, one of the oldest and largest covered markets in the world."

Creating a Packing List

Forgetting essential items can be a hassle during travel. ChatGPT can help you create a customized packing list based on your destination, the season, and planned activities. This ensures you have everything you need, from clothing and toiletries to travel documents and gadgets.

Example:

"I'm going hiking in the Swiss Alps in summer. What should I pack?"

Response: "For a summer hike in the Swiss Alps, pack lightweight, breathable clothing, a sturdy pair of hiking boots, a waterproof jacket, sunscreen, a hat, a refillable water bottle, and a small first-aid kit. Don't forget your camera to capture the stunning views!"

Conclusion

Using ChatGPT as your travel planner can simplify every step of your journey, from finding the perfect destination to crafting an itinerary that matches your interests. With its help, you can spend less time stressing over details and more time enjoying your adventures. Whether you're a seasoned traveler or planning your first big trip, ChatGPT can be your go-to resource for making every vacation a memorable experience.

Chapter 9:
Staying Connected with Family Using ChatGPT

In today's busy world, staying connected with family can sometimes be challenging. Whether you're living far away or just caught up in the hustle and bustle of daily life, it's important to maintain those precious connections with loved ones. ChatGPT can help you draft heartwarming messages, create family newsletters, and write personalized letters that make staying in touch easy and meaningful. This chapter explores how to use ChatGPT to keep your family bonds strong and vibrant.

Writing Heartfelt Messages

Sometimes, finding the right words to express your feelings can be difficult, especially when you want to show appreciation or offer support. ChatGPT can help you craft thoughtful and sincere messages for various occasions, from birthdays and anniversaries to simple "thinking of you" notes.

Example:

"I want to send a message to my sister just to let her know I'm thinking of her."

Response: "Hey [Sister's Name], I've been thinking about you a lot lately. I hope you're doing well and taking some time for yourself. Just wanted to remind you how much you mean to me and that I'm always here if you need anything. Love you!"

You can also use ChatGPT to tailor messages for special events, adding a personal touch that makes your loved ones feel valued and remembered.

Example:

"Can you help me write a birthday message for my dad?"

Response: "Happy Birthday, Dad! ◈ You've always been my rock and my inspiration. I'm so grateful for everything you've taught me and the love you've given me over the years. Wishing you a wonderful day filled with joy and laughter. Here's to many more amazing years together!"

Creating Family Newsletters

Family newsletters are a wonderful way to keep everyone updated on what's happening in each other's lives, especially when relatives are spread out across the country or even the world. ChatGPT can help you create engaging newsletters that share family news, upcoming events, and even photos or stories from recent gatherings.

Example:

"I want to start a family newsletter. How can I format it?"

Response:

"Here's a simple structure for your family newsletter:

1. Welcome Note: A warm greeting and a brief introduction.
2. Family Highlights: Updates on significant events like graduations, new jobs, or family vacations.
3. Upcoming Events: Information about birthdays, anniversaries, or planned family get-togethers.
4. Photo Section: A few pictures from recent family gatherings or special moments.
5. Closing Message: A few kind words to wrap up the newsletter,

perhaps with a fun fact or family trivia."

Using ChatGPT to draft content for each section can make the process quicker and ensure your newsletters are both informative and enjoyable to read.

Writing Letters to Loved Ones

Whether it's a heartfelt letter to grandparents or a simple note to a distant cousin, writing letters is a timeless way to show you care. ChatGPT can assist in structuring your thoughts and adding the right emotional tone to your letters, making them more personal and impactful.
Example:
"I want to write a letter to my grandparents, but I'm not sure what to say."
Response:
"Dear Grandma and Grandpa,
I hope this letter finds you both in good health and spirits. I've been thinking a lot about the summer holidays we used to spend together and how much I miss those days. You've always been such an important part of my life, and I cherish every moment we've shared. I'm looking forward to visiting you soon and catching up. Please take care and know that I'm always thinking of you.
With love, [Your Name]."
By using ChatGPT to draft your letters, you can ensure they express your feelings sincerely and leave a lasting impression on the reader.

Conclusion

Staying connected with family doesn't have to be complicated or time-consuming. With ChatGPT, you can easily craft heartfelt messages, create engaging family newsletters, and write thoughtful letters that bring your loved ones closer, no matter the distance. By making communication easier and more meaningful, ChatGPT helps you nurture and strengthen your family bonds, keeping the love and connection alive.

Chapter 10:
Using ChatGPT for Health and Wellness

Maintaining good health is essential, especially as we age. For seniors, keeping track of health routines, staying active, and staying motivated can sometimes be challenging. ChatGPT can play a valuable role in supporting health and wellness by offering gentle reminders, sharing wellness tips, and sending motivational messages to keep you engaged and focused on your well-being. This chapter explores practical ways seniors can use ChatGPT to support their health and wellness goals, making daily routines easier and more enjoyable.

1. Setting Medication and Appointment Reminders

Remembering to take medication or attend doctor's appointments is crucial for maintaining good health, but it can be easy to forget these tasks, especially if you have a busy schedule or multiple prescriptions. ChatGPT can help set up reminders so you never miss a dose or an appointment.

Example:

"ChatGPT, remind me to take my blood pressure medication at 8:00 AM every day."

Response: "Sure! I'll remind you to take your blood pressure medication every morning at 8:00 AM."

You can also ask ChatGPT to remind you of upcoming medical appointments, such as check-ups or specialist visits, helping you stay organized and punctual.

Example:

"I have a doctor's appointment next Wednesday. Can you remind me a day before?"

Response: "I'll remind you on Tuesday to get ready for your doctor's appointment on Wednesday."

2. Wellness Tips for Daily Routines

Staying healthy involves more than just taking medication; it also means eating well, staying active, and taking care of your mental health. ChatGPT can provide simple, effective wellness tips to incorporate into your daily routines. Whether you need advice on what to eat for breakfast or tips for gentle exercises, ChatGPT has you covered.

Example:

"What are some healthy breakfast ideas for seniors?"

Response: "A healthy breakfast could include:

- Oatmeal topped with fresh berries and a sprinkle of nuts.

- Scrambled eggs with spinach and whole-grain toast.

- Greek yogurt with sliced banana and a drizzle of honey.

These options provide a good balance of protein, fiber, and healthy fats to start your day right."

If you're looking to add more movement to your day, ChatGPT can suggest simple exercises that are easy to do at home.

Example:

"What are some easy exercises I can do at home?"

Response: "Here are some gentle exercises you can try:

- Chair Yoga: Sit in a sturdy chair and stretch your arms, legs, and back.

- Walking in Place: March in place for a few minutes while watching TV or listening to music.

- Leg Lifts: While seated, lift one leg at a time, holding for a few seconds before switching.

These activities can help improve flexibility, strength, and circulation."

3. Motivational Messages for Staying Active and Positive

Staying motivated, especially on challenging days, can make a big difference in achieving wellness goals. ChatGPT can send encouraging messages and reminders to help you stay positive and active. You can set up daily motivational quotes or personalized messages that inspire you to keep going, even when you don't feel like it.

Example:

"Can you send me a daily motivational message to help me stay active?"

Response: "Of course! Here's your message for today: 'Every step you take is a step toward a healthier you. Keep moving, and remember that small efforts add up to big results!' I'll send you a new message each day to keep you inspired."

4. Tracking Wellness Goals

Setting and tracking wellness goals, such as increasing daily steps or drinking more water, can help you stay focused and make progress over time. ChatGPT can help you set realistic goals and remind you to track your achievements regularly.

Example:

"I want to drink more water every day. Can you help me track it?"

Response: "Let's set a goal! How about aiming for 8 glasses of water a day? I'll remind you to log your water intake, and we can check in at the end of the day to see how you did."

By keeping track of your progress, ChatGPT helps you stay accountable and motivated, making it easier to develop healthy habits over time.

5. Learning About Health Topics

Staying informed about health topics is an important part of wellness. ChatGPT can provide information on various health issues, such as managing blood pressure, understanding nutrition labels, or learning about mental wellness techniques.

Example:

"What are some tips for managing high blood pressure?"

Response: "To help manage high blood pressure, try these tips:

- Reduce salt intake by avoiding processed and canned foods.

- Include potassium-rich foods like bananas, sweet potatoes, and spinach in your diet.

- Aim for 30 minutes of moderate exercise, such as brisk walking, most days of the week.

- Practice relaxation techniques like deep breathing or meditation to reduce stress.

Always consult your doctor for personalized advice."

6. Staying Social and Engaged

Staying connected with others is vital for mental and emotional health. ChatGPT can help you plan virtual meet-ups with family, suggest hobbies or clubs to join, or even guide you in setting up video calls to stay in touch with loved ones.

Example:

"I'd like to stay in touch with my grandkids. Any ideas?"

Response: "How about scheduling a weekly video call to catch up and maybe even read a story together? You can also try sharing photos or short video messages throughout the week to stay connected."

Conclusion

Using ChatGPT for health and wellness support can make a big difference in staying organized, motivated, and informed. From reminders and wellness tips to motivational messages and health information, ChatGPT offers a practical and accessible way to enhance your well-being. By integrating these simple tools into your daily routine, you can take proactive steps toward maintaining a healthy and fulfilling lifestyle.

Chapter 11:
Managing Finances with ChatGPT

Managing personal finances can sometimes feel overwhelming, especially when balancing a budget, tracking expenses, and making informed financial decisions. ChatGPT can be a helpful companion in this process, offering guidance, answering questions, and helping you stay on top of your financial goals. This chapter explores practical ways to use ChatGPT to budget effectively, monitor spending, and gain a better understanding of personal finance—all in an easy and accessible way.

1. Creating a Budget

One of the foundational steps to managing your finances is creating a budget. A budget helps you plan how to spend your money each month, ensuring you cover essential expenses and save for future goals. ChatGPT can assist in setting up a basic budget by breaking down your income and expenses into categories.

Example:

"Can you help me create a monthly budget?"

Response: "Of course! Let's start with your monthly income. Then, we'll divide your expenses into categories like housing, utilities, groceries, transportation, and entertainment. For example:

- Income: $2,500

- Housing (Rent/Mortgage): $900

- Utilities (Electricity, Water, Internet): $150

- Groceries: $300

- Transportation: $100

- Entertainment: $100

This leaves you with $950 for savings or additional expenses. Would you like to adjust any of these categories?"

Once your budget is set up, ChatGPT can remind you to review and adjust it regularly, ensuring that it remains aligned with your financial goals.

2. Tracking Expenses

Keeping track of where your money goes is crucial to sticking to your budget. ChatGPT can help you monitor your spending habits by categorizing and summarizing your expenses. You can either manually input your expenses or use ChatGPT as a guide to set up an expense-tracking system.

Example:

"I want to track my expenses. How should I start?"

Response: "A good way to track your expenses is to note down each purchase in a notebook or a budgeting app. For example, list out your daily expenses like:

- Groceries: $45

- Gas: $30

- Dining out: $20

At the end of the week or month, categorize these expenses into groups like Food, Transportation, and Entertainment. This will help you see where most of your money is going and where you can cut back if needed."

ChatGPT can also remind you to review your expenses at the end of each week or month, helping you stay aware of your spending patterns.

3. Asking Financial Questions

When it comes to personal finance, there are often many questions, from understanding credit scores to learning about investment options. While ChatGPT cannot offer specific financial advice, it can provide general information and resources to help you make informed decisions.

Example:

"What is a credit score, and why is it important?"

Response: "A credit score is a numerical representation of your creditworthiness, ranging from 300 to 850. It's based on factors like your payment history, the amount of debt you have, and the length of your credit history. A higher score can help you get better interest rates on loans and credit cards. It's important to pay bills on time and keep credit card balances low to maintain a good score."

Example:

"What's the difference between a Roth IRA and a Traditional IRA?"

Response: "A Traditional IRA allows you to make pre-tax contributions, which reduces your taxable income in the year you contribute, but you'll pay taxes when you withdraw in retirement. A Roth IRA, on the other hand, is funded with after-tax dollars, so withdrawals in retirement are tax-free. The choice between them depends on whether you expect to be in a higher or lower tax bracket in the future."

4. Setting Financial Goals

Whether you're saving for a vacation, a new car, or retirement, setting clear financial goals is essential. ChatGPT can help you define your goals, set realistic timelines, and track your progress.

Example:

"I want to save $5,000 for a vacation next year. How much should I save each month?"

Response: "To save $5,000 in one year, you would need to save about $417 each month. If this amount feels too high, consider extending your timeline or finding ways to cut back on other expenses to reach your goal more comfortably."

ChatGPT can also provide tips on how to achieve your goals faster, such as cutting unnecessary subscriptions or finding ways to increase your income through side gigs or hobbies.

5. Managing Debt and Building Savings

If you're dealing with debt, ChatGPT can suggest strategies for paying it off efficiently, such as focusing on high-interest debts first (the avalanche method) or tackling smaller debts to build momentum (the snowball method). For savings, ChatGPT can offer advice on building an emergency fund or finding high-yield savings accounts.

Example:

"I have credit card debt and a car loan. How should I pay them off?"

Response: "Consider the avalanche method: prioritize paying off the debt with the highest interest rate first, while making minimum payments on the others. This way, you'll save on interest over time. If you prefer small wins, the snowball method might work better, where you pay off the smallest debt first, then move on to the next."

6. Staying Motivated

Managing finances can sometimes feel like a daunting task, but staying motivated is key to reaching your goals. ChatGPT can send motivational messages or reminders to keep you focused and positive about your financial journey.

Example:

"Can you help keep me motivated to save?"

Response: "Absolutely! Remember, every dollar saved brings you closer to your goal. Keep picturing yourself enjoying that vacation or reaching a debt-free milestone. I'll remind you to check in on your progress each week!"

Conclusion

Managing finances doesn't have to be stressful or confusing. With ChatGPT's support, you can create a budget, track your expenses, set financial goals, and get answers to your finance-related questions. By integrating these simple tools and strategies into your daily routine, you can gain more control over your financial future and make informed decisions with confidence.

Chapter 12:

Exploring Entertainment with ChatGPT

Finding new entertainment options that match your tastes can sometimes be a challenge. With so many choices out there, it's easy to feel overwhelmed. ChatGPT can help you navigate the world of entertainment by recommending music, books, TV shows, and movies based on your personal preferences. In this chapter, we'll explore how you can use ChatGPT to discover new favorites in each of these categories, making it easier to enjoy your leisure time.

1. Discovering New Music

Whether you're into classic rock, jazz, or the latest pop hits, ChatGPT can suggest songs and artists that match your musical tastes. You can ask for recommendations based on your favorite genres, artists, or even specific moods.

Example:

"I'm a big fan of 70s rock. Can you suggest some songs or bands I might like?"

Response: "If you love 70s rock, you might enjoy bands like Fleetwood Mac, Led Zeppelin, and The Eagles. For specific songs, try 'Go Your Own Way' by Fleetwood Mac, 'Stairway to Heaven' by Led Zeppelin, and 'Hotel California' by The Eagles."

You can also ask for music based on specific themes or activities, such as workout playlists or relaxing tunes for unwinding after a long day.

Example:

"Can you suggest some relaxing music to listen to before bed?"

Response: "Sure! Try listening to calming artists like Norah Jones, Enya, or instrumental piano music by Ludovico Einaudi. Songs like 'Come Away with Me' by Norah Jones or 'Watermark' by Enya can help you relax and unwind."

2. Finding Your Next Great Read

If you're looking for a new book to dive into, ChatGPT can recommend titles based on your favorite genres, authors, or themes. Whether you love mystery novels, historical fiction, or self-help books, ChatGPT can point you toward your next great read.

Example:

"I just finished reading 'The Da Vinci Code.' Can you suggest a similar book?"

Response: "If you enjoyed 'The Da Vinci Code,' you might like 'Angels & Demons,' also by Dan Brown. For similar themes of historical intrigue and conspiracy, try 'The Eight' by Katherine Neville or 'The Lost Symbol' by Dan Brown."

You can also explore different genres or ask for books that focus on specific topics or life experiences.

Example:

"I'm interested in reading books about personal growth. Any recommendations?"

Response: "For personal growth, I recommend 'Atomic Habits' by James Clear for building good habits, 'The Power of Now' by Eckhart Tolle for mindfulness and presence, and 'Daring Greatly' by Brené Brown for learning about vulnerability and courage."

3. Discovering TV Shows and Movies

Finding the right TV show or movie to watch can take up more time than actually watching it! ChatGPT can help narrow down your options based on your preferred genres, favorite actors, or even current mood.

Example:

"I love crime dramas. What TV shows would you suggest?"

Response: "If you're into crime dramas, you might enjoy 'Mindhunter,' which delves into the early days of FBI criminal profiling, or 'Broadchurch,' a British series about a small town rocked by a tragic crime. 'True Detective' is another great choice, featuring complex characters and gripping stories."

For movie buffs, ChatGPT can recommend films based on your favorite genres or suggest something new to match your mood, from comedies and thrillers to documentaries and animated features.

Example:

"I'm in the mood for a feel-good movie. What do you recommend?"

Response: "For a feel-good movie, try 'The Intouchables,' a heartwarming French film about an unlikely friendship, or 'Forrest Gump,' which tells the inspiring story of a man's incredible life journey. 'The Secret Life of Walter Mitty' is another uplifting choice that encourages you to step out of your comfort zone."

4. Exploring New Hobbies and Interests

Beyond traditional entertainment, ChatGPT can also suggest new hobbies or interests to explore. If you're looking to learn something new or pick up a new skill, ChatGPT can provide ideas and resources to get started.

Example:

"I want to try a new hobby. Any suggestions?"

Response: "How about trying something creative like painting or photography? If you prefer something more active, you could explore hiking or yoga. For a relaxing indoor hobby, consider starting a collection, like stamps or vintage postcards, or learning to play a musical instrument."

ChatGPT can also offer recommendations for educational content, such as documentaries, podcasts, or online courses that align with your interests.

Example:

"I'd like to learn more about world history. What are some good documentaries to watch?"

Response: "For world history, I recommend 'The World Wars,' which covers the major events and figures of the 20th century, and 'Civilisations,' which explores the development of art and culture throughout history. 'The Story of China' is another excellent series that delves into China's rich and complex past."

5. Personalizing Your Entertainment Experience

One of the best ways to use ChatGPT is to get personalized recommendations that are tailored to your specific preferences. The more you share about your likes and dislikes, the better ChatGPT can refine its suggestions, making your entertainment experience truly unique and enjoyable.

Example:

"I loved 'Stranger Things' and 'The X-Files.' What else would I like?"

Response: "If you enjoyed the mix of supernatural elements and mystery in 'Stranger Things' and 'The X-Files,' you might like 'Dark,' a German series with a complex, time-traveling storyline, or 'Twin Peaks,' which combines eerie small-town drama with supernatural intrigue."

Conclusion

ChatGPT can be your personal entertainment guide, helping you discover new music, books, TV shows, and movies that perfectly match your tastes. By exploring different genres and interests, you can enrich your leisure time and find joy in new and unexpected places. Whether you're looking for a captivating novel, an exciting new series, or just some relaxing music, ChatGPT is here to make finding your next favorite pastime easier and more enjoyable.

Chapter 13:
Getting Technical Help with ChatGPT

Technology is a big part of our daily lives, but it can sometimes be tricky to navigate. From troubleshooting tech issues to learning how to use new apps or solving minor problems, it's not always easy to know where to start. ChatGPT can be a helpful assistant for handling these technical challenges, offering simple and clear guidance to help you overcome tech-related hurdles. In this chapter, we'll explore how ChatGPT can assist with troubleshooting, learning new technologies, and resolving minor tech issues—all in a way that's easy to understand and follow.

1. Troubleshooting Common Tech Issues

When your computer, smartphone, or other devices don't work as expected, it can be frustrating. ChatGPT can help you troubleshoot common problems like slow performance, connectivity issues, or software glitches. By providing step-by-step instructions, it can guide you through resolving these issues.

Example:

"My laptop is running very slowly. Can you help?"

Response: "Sure! Here are a few steps you can try:

1. Restart Your Laptop: Sometimes a simple restart can fix performance issues.
2. Check for Updates: Make sure your operating system and apps are up-to-date. Go to Settings > Update & Security and check for updates.
3. Clear Temporary Files: Use a tool like Disk Cleanup on Windows or delete cache files on a Mac to free up space.
4. Check Background Processes: Press Ctrl + Shift + Esc to open Task Manager (Windows) or Command + Option + Esc for Activity Monitor (Mac). Close any unnecessary apps that are using a lot of resources.

Try these steps and let me know if the performance improves!"

2. Learning How to Use New Apps or Features

Learning new software or features can be overwhelming, especially with constant updates and changes. ChatGPT can provide clear and concise instructions on how to use new apps or features, helping you get up to speed quickly.

Example:

"I just got a new iPhone. How do I set up the Face ID?"

Response: "To set up Face ID on your iPhone, follow these steps:

1. Go to Settings > Face ID & Passcode.
2. Tap Set Up Face ID.
3. Hold your device in portrait mode and position your face in front of the camera.
4. Move your head in a circle to complete the scan.
5. Tap Continue and repeat the process.

6. Once completed, tap Done.
   Your Face ID is now set up and ready to use!"

You can also ask ChatGPT how to perform specific actions in popular apps like managing contacts, sending emails, or using new features in social media platforms.

Example:

"How do I create a new contact in Gmail?"

Response: "To create a new contact in Gmail:

1. Open Gmail and click on the Google Apps icon (nine dots) in the upper right corner.
2. Select Contacts from the menu.
3. Click the Create Contact button.
4. Enter the contact's name, email, and any other information you want to include.
5. Click Save.
   Your new contact will now be saved in your Google Contacts list."

3. Solving Minor Tech Problems

Sometimes small tech issues, like connecting a printer or setting up Wi-Fi, can turn into big headaches. ChatGPT can provide quick solutions to these common problems, saving you time and frustration.

Example:

"I'm having trouble connecting my printer to my Wi-Fi network. What should I do?"

Response: "Here's how to connect your printer to Wi-Fi:

1. Make sure your printer is powered on and near your Wi-Fi router.
2. On the printer's control panel, go to Settings or Network Settings.
3. Select Wireless Setup Wizard and choose your Wi-Fi network from the list.
4. Enter your Wi-Fi password and confirm the connection.
5. Once connected, try printing a test page.

If you still have issues, restart both your printer and router, and try the setup again."

If you're not sure what's causing the issue, ChatGPT can help you troubleshoot by asking a series of questions to narrow down the problem and suggest appropriate steps.

Example:
"My Wi-Fi keeps disconnecting. What could be the problem?"
Response: "There could be a few reasons for Wi-Fi disconnections:

1. Router Placement: Make sure your router is in a central location, away from obstructions and electronic devices that can cause interference.
2. Network Congestion: If multiple devices are using the Wi-Fi simultaneously, it can slow down the connection. Try disconnecting some devices.
3. Outdated Firmware: Check if your router has any firmware updates. Visit the manufacturer's website for instructions.
4. Signal Strength: If the signal is weak, consider using a Wi-Fi extender or moving closer to the router.
   Try these solutions and see if the connection improves!"

4. Getting Advice on Buying New Devices

If you're considering purchasing a new gadget, ChatGPT can help you understand the key features and make a more informed decision. Whether you're looking at smartphones, tablets, or home tech devices, ChatGPT can provide comparisons and insights based on your needs and budget.

Example:
"I'm thinking of buying a new tablet. What should I look for?"
Response: "When choosing a tablet, consider the following factors:

1. Operating System: Decide between iOS (Apple iPad), Android, or Windows based on your preferences and the apps you plan to use.
2. Screen Size and Resolution: A larger screen is great for media

consumption, while a smaller one is more portable. Look for at least Full HD resolution for sharp images.

3. Storage and RAM: Choose a tablet with at least 4GB of RAM for smooth performance and enough storage to meet your needs (32GB or more).

4. Battery Life: Look for a battery life of at least 8-10 hours for all-day use.

5. Additional Features: Consider if you need features like a stylus, keyboard compatibility, or a high-quality camera.

    Think about what's most important to you, and I can help you compare models!"

5. Understanding Tech Terms and Concepts

Tech jargon can be confusing, but ChatGPT can explain technical terms and concepts in simple language. This is useful if you want to understand how something works or what certain features mean.

Example:

"What is the cloud, and how does it work?"

Response: "The 'cloud' refers to servers that are accessed over the internet, along with the software and databases that run on those servers. Instead of storing files on your computer, you can save them to the cloud, which allows you to access them from any device with an internet connection. It's a way to store and share data without using up space on your own devices."

Conclusion

With ChatGPT, tackling tech issues doesn't have to be a daunting task. From troubleshooting problems to learning new apps and understanding tech terms, ChatGPT can provide clear, step-by-step assistance that makes technology more accessible. Whether you're resolving a minor glitch or exploring new features on your devices, ChatGPT is here to help you feel more confident and capable in managing your digital world.

Chapter 14:
Keeping a Memory Journal with ChatGPT

Recording and preserving memories is a beautiful way to reflect on your life and share your experiences with loved ones. Whether you're documenting significant life events, recounting everyday moments, or capturing family stories, a memory journal can be a treasured keepsake. ChatGPT can help you create and maintain this journal, making it easy to organize and express your thoughts. In this chapter, we'll explore how to use ChatGPT to record your memories, write personal stories, and keep a detailed account of your life's journey.

1. Documenting Daily Moments

One of the simplest ways to start a memory journal is by recording daily moments that stand out. These can be small, everyday experiences that bring joy, such as a pleasant walk, a conversation with a friend, or even your thoughts on a favorite book or movie. ChatGPT can help you capture these details and create a meaningful record of your day-to-day life.

Example:

"Today, I spent the afternoon in the garden. Can you help me write about it?"

Response: "Certainly! Here's a suggestion:

'This afternoon was spent among the flowers in my garden. The sun was warm, and a gentle breeze rustled the leaves. I planted new roses and enjoyed the vibrant colors of the blooms. It was a peaceful time, filled with the simple pleasure of being outdoors and feeling connected to nature.'"

By capturing these small moments, you create a journal that not only documents events but also reflects your feelings and thoughts.

2. Preserving Life Stories

Everyone has unique life experiences and stories worth preserving. Whether it's childhood memories, tales of family traditions, or significant life events, ChatGPT can help you write these stories in a structured and engaging way. This can be especially valuable for sharing your personal history with future generations.

Example:

"I want to write about the day I moved into my first home. Can you help me get started?"

Response: "Of course! Here's a starting point:

'Moving into my first home was a day filled with excitement and a touch of nervousness. I remember carrying boxes up the stairs, feeling a sense of accomplishment with each step. The rooms were empty, but they were full of promise. I could already picture how I would arrange the furniture and make this place my own. That first night, I sat on the floor with a cup of tea, surrounded by unpacked boxes, feeling both proud and at peace.'"

You can continue adding details, such as how you chose the home, memorable moments during the move, and your feelings as you settled in, creating a vivid and personal story.

3. Capturing Family Memories

Family memories, from holiday traditions to shared vacations, are often the most cherished. ChatGPT can help you document these special moments in a way that highlights the love and connection within your family. You can write about favorite family recipes, funny anecdotes, or the significance of certain family rituals.

Example:

"Can you help me write about our family's Thanksgiving tradition?"

Response: "Sure! How about this:

'Every Thanksgiving, our family gathers around a long, wooden table, set with dishes that have been passed down for generations. We start the day early, each of us contributing to the meal in our own way—Grandma making her famous stuffing, Dad roasting the turkey, and the kids helping to set the table. After the meal, we always take a walk together, enjoying the crisp autumn air and each other's company. It's a day not just of food, but of family and gratitude, a tradition that reminds us of the ties that bind us.'"

These stories can be compiled into a family memory journal that serves as a cherished heirloom.

4. Reflecting on Personal Growth and Experiences

Keeping a memory journal can also be a powerful tool for self-reflection. You can use ChatGPT to write about your personal growth, the lessons you've learned, and how you've changed over time. This type of journaling helps you gain perspective on your life and appreciate the journey you've been on.

Example:

"I want to write about how I've changed over the years. Can you help?"

Response: "Here's a possible reflection:

'Looking back, I see how much I've grown. I used to be more hesitant, unsure of my choices, but over the years, I've become more confident and comfortable in my own skin. I've learned to trust myself, to speak up when it matters, and to embrace both the highs and the lows of life. Each challenge has shaped me, each success has encouraged me, and I am grateful for the person I've become.'"

This kind of reflection not only captures who you are today but also honors your past and the experiences that have contributed to your growth.

5. Creating a Digital Memory Journal

If you prefer a digital format, ChatGPT can help you organize your memories in a way that's easy to navigate. You can create categories such as "Childhood," "Family Holidays," or "Life Lessons," and ChatGPT can assist in formatting and organizing your entries.

Example:

"I want to create sections in my memory journal for different life stages. How should I organize it?"

Response: "You can structure your journal with these sections:

1. Early Years: Memories from your childhood, family traditions, and first experiences.
2. Adolescence: School days, friendships, challenges, and achievements during your teenage years.
3. Adulthood: Career milestones, personal growth, and important relationships.
4. Family Life: Stories of raising children, family vacations, and special moments.
5. Reflections: Lessons learned, personal growth, and thoughts on life's journey.
   This organization helps you easily find and add memories as they come to mind."

6. Sharing Your Stories

Once you've created a collection of memories, you might want to share them with family members or friends. ChatGPT can help you format your stories into a book or a digital document, making it easy to share your experiences with others.

Example:

"I'd like to share my memory journal with my family. How should I format it?"

Response: "Consider creating a digital document or a printed booklet. Use each section or chapter to highlight different themes or life stages. Include photos if possible, and add a personal note at the beginning, explaining why you've created this journal and what these memories mean to you."

Conclusion

Keeping a memory journal with ChatGPT is a wonderful way to preserve your personal history and share your life stories. Whether you're capturing everyday moments or reflecting on significant events, ChatGPT can help you express your thoughts clearly and beautifully. By documenting your experiences, you create a lasting legacy that honors your journey and connects you with the people you care about.

Chapter 15:
Using ChatGPT for Stress Management – The Power of Organization

Stress has a way of sneaking into our lives, especially when we're overwhelmed with tasks, responsibilities, and constant pressure. Whether it's managing work deadlines, running a household, or simply trying to keep track of daily commitments, things can pile up quickly. The good news? You don't have to tackle it all on your own. One simple yet powerful strategy for stress management is organization, and ChatGPT can be your go-to tool in this journey.

Let's explore how keeping life organized can help reduce stress and how ChatGPT can assist you in calming the chaos.

Why an Organized Life is a Stress-Free Life

Imagine walking into a cluttered room versus a neat, well-arranged space. Which one makes you feel calmer? It's the same with your mind. When your tasks, priorities, and thoughts are all over the place, it's easy to feel overwhelmed. However, when things are organized, you gain clarity, control, and the ability to handle life's demands without getting bogged down.

Here are a few ways an organized life can lower stress:

- Clarity: You know exactly what you need to do and when.
- Control: You avoid the feeling of being pulled in a million directions.
- Confidence: Knowing what's next helps you approach challenges calmly.
- Time Management: You have a plan, so you use your time efficiently.

In short, organization creates a sense of order in both your environment and mind, helping to prevent stress from spiraling out of control.

How ChatGPT Can Help You Get Organized

ChatGPT is like having a personal assistant right at your fingertips, 24/7. Whether it's helping you plan your day, breaking down overwhelming tasks, or suggesting stress management techniques, ChatGPT can be an invaluable resource. Let's dive into specific ways you can use ChatGPT to stay organized and stress-free.

1. Creating To-Do Lists

When your mind is racing with all the things you need to get done, a to-do list can bring instant relief. But sometimes, figuring out where to start can be a challenge in itself. Here's where ChatGPT steps in. You can ask ChatGPT to help create a simple, structured to-do list. For example:

You: *I have so many things to do today, but I don't know where to start. Can you help me organize my tasks?*

ChatGPT: *Of course! Let's break it down. Can you tell me what you need to accomplish today?*

With ChatGPT's help, you'll soon have a clear list of tasks, from most urgent to least important. This makes it easier to focus on one thing at a time instead of being overwhelmed by everything at once.

2. Prioritizing Tasks

Not all tasks are created equal. Some require immediate attention, while others can wait. By prioritizing your tasks, you can focus on what really matters, leaving the less important things for later. ChatGPT can help you decide which tasks should come first based on urgency or time sensitivity.

You: *I have a project due in three days, but I also need to run errands and answer emails. What should I focus on first?*

ChatGPT: *Start with your project since it has a deadline. Set aside specific times later in the day for emails and errands. That way, you're staying productive without feeling rushed.*

By prioritizing, you avoid the stress of last-minute scrambles and can work through your list more efficiently.

3. Breaking Down Big Tasks into Manageable Steps

Sometimes, a single large task can feel intimidating. For example, if you're working on a project that's due soon, the sheer size of the work can be paralyzing. Instead of staring blankly at your screen, ask ChatGPT to break the task down into smaller, manageable steps.

You: *I'm feeling overwhelmed by my big presentation. How do I even start?*

ChatGPT: *Let's break it into steps. First, gather all your research materials. Next, outline your main points. After that, create slides for each point. Finally, rehearse your presentation a couple of times.*

Step-by-step guidance makes it easier to start and maintain momentum. You'll soon notice that what once felt overwhelming is now more manageable and less stressful.

4. Suggesting Time Management Techniques

One of the main causes of stress is the feeling that there's not enough time in the day. Fortunately, ChatGPT is full of time management techniques to help you maximize your productivity. Whether it's the Pomodoro technique (working in timed intervals), setting specific time blocks for tasks, or creating deadlines for yourself, ChatGPT can suggest ways to make the most of your time.

You: *I keep procrastinating on my work. Do you have any tips for staying focused?*

ChatGPT: *Try the Pomodoro technique: work for 25 minutes, then take a 5-minute break. After four sessions, take a longer break. This can help you stay focused without feeling overwhelmed.*

These strategies help you stay on task and prevent time from slipping away, making you feel more in control and less stressed.

5. Promoting Relaxation and Mindfulness

Organization isn't just about ticking things off your to-do list—it's also about making time for yourself. ChatGPT can offer suggestions for mindfulness exercises, relaxation techniques, or even fun activities to help you recharge.

You: *I've been stressed all day. Any suggestions to help me relax?*

ChatGPT: *Try a quick 5-minute breathing exercise. Sit in a quiet place, close your eyes, and take slow, deep breaths. Focus on each breath as you inhale and exhale. You can also try journaling your thoughts to clear your mind.*

By incorporating relaxation into your day, you can prevent stress from building up and stay calm in the face of challenges.

Conclusion: Calm the Chaos with ChatGPT

An organized life is a calmer life, and with ChatGPT by your side, you don't have to face the chaos alone. By using ChatGPT to create to-do lists, prioritize tasks, break down overwhelming projects, and suggest time management strategies, you can take control of your day and approach your responsibilities with clarity and confidence.

Remember, stress doesn't have to rule your life. A little organization goes a long way in creating a peaceful mind—and with ChatGPT, staying organized is easier than ever.

Chapter 16:
Using ChatGPT for Fun and Games – Let the Play Begin!

Who said technology has to be all work and no play? While ChatGPT can help you stay organized and manage stress, it's also a great companion for fun activities! Whether you want to challenge yourself with trivia, test your skills with word games, or even create personalized puzzles, ChatGPT offers a world of entertainment right at your fingertips.

In this chapter, we'll explore some playful ways to engage with ChatGPT, helping you bring creativity and joy into your daily routine.

Why Fun Matters in Daily Life

Play isn't just for kids—it's essential for all of us. Engaging in fun activities keeps our minds sharp, reduces stress, and adds a spark of happiness to everyday life. Whether you're looking for a quick mental break, a way to unwind, or just something different to do, ChatGPT can help you get there.

Here are a few benefits of making time for fun:

- **Mental stimulation:** Games like trivia and puzzles challenge your brain in new ways.

- **Relaxation:** Fun activities are a great way to unwind and take your mind off worries.

- **Creativity:** Playing with language and ideas keeps your creativity flowing.

- **Social engagement:** Many games can be shared with family or friends, offering a chance to connect.

Now, let's dive into how you can use ChatGPT to turn everyday moments into playful, engaging experiences.

1. Playing Word Games with ChatGPT

Word games are a fantastic way to keep your brain active, and ChatGPT can play along with you! Whether you enjoy classic games like 20 Questions or want to try something new, ChatGPT makes it easy to engage in quick, fun challenges that sharpen your thinking.

Example: Word Guessing Game

You can ask ChatGPT to play a word guessing game with you. Here's how:

You: *Let's play a word guessing game! I'm thinking of a word. You have to guess it.*

ChatGPT: *Great! Is it a person, place, or thing?*

From there, you can give ChatGPT clues, and it will try to guess the word. Or, you can reverse roles and have ChatGPT think of a word, while you ask yes-or-no questions to figure it out. Games like this are a fun way to pass the time and keep your mind engaged.

Example: Riddles

If you're in the mood for a brain teaser, ask ChatGPT to give you a riddle. Here's how it might go:

You: *Give me a riddle to solve!*

ChatGPT: *Sure! I speak without a mouth and hear without ears. I have no body, but I come alive with the wind. What am I?*

You: *Hmm, that's tricky... is it an echo?*

ChatGPT: *Correct!*

These quick games help keep your mind active and entertained, perfect for those moments when you want a little mental challenge.

2. Challenging Yourself with Trivia

Who doesn't love testing their knowledge with a good trivia challenge? Whether you're a history buff, a movie lover, or a science fan, ChatGPT can generate trivia questions that suit your interests. This can be a solo activity or something you share with friends or family.

Example: General Trivia

You can ask ChatGPT to quiz you on any topic you like. Here's an example:

You: *I want to play trivia! Can you quiz me on history?*

ChatGPT: *Sure! Here's your first question: Who was the first president of the United States?*

You: *George Washington!*

ChatGPT: *Correct! Ready for the next one?*

You can play as long as you like, switching topics when you want. It's a fun way to test your knowledge and learn something new along the way.

Example: Custom Trivia Games

You can even ask ChatGPT to create a custom trivia game for you, where you set the rules or topics. Want a game based on your favorite TV show? Or trivia about world capitals? ChatGPT can generate questions that match your interests, making the game even more enjoyable and personalized.

You: *Can you create trivia questions about classic movies?*

ChatGPT: *Absolutely! Here's one: In which 1942 movie does the line "Here's looking at you, kid" appear?*

You: *That's easy! Casablanca.*

This personalized approach ensures that you're not only having fun but also engaging with topics you love.

3. Generating Personalized Puzzles

Puzzles are another fantastic way to stay mentally sharp and entertained. From crosswords to logic puzzles, ChatGPT can create custom challenges that keep your brain working. You can ask for puzzles suited to your difficulty level or request specific types of puzzles based on what you enjoy.

Example: Crossword Clues

You can ask ChatGPT to generate crossword-style clues for you to solve.

You: *Can you give me some crossword puzzle clues?*

ChatGPT: *Sure! Here's your first clue: "A four-letter word for a large body of water."*

You: *That must be "sea"!*

ChatGPT can provide as many clues as you want, creating a fun and challenging mini-crossword session right on the spot.

Example: Logic Puzzles

If you enjoy logic puzzles, ChatGPT can generate those too. For example:

You: *Give me a logic puzzle to solve.*

ChatGPT: *Okay! Three friends, Anna, Ben, and Charlie, each have a different favorite color: red, blue, and green. Anna does not like red. Ben's favorite color is not blue. What is each person's favorite color?*

Solving puzzles like these gives your brain a workout while offering a sense of accomplishment when you find the solution.

4. Creative Writing Games

If you're feeling imaginative, why not engage ChatGPT in a creative writing game? This can be as simple as asking it to help you write a story together, where you take turns adding to the narrative, or playing a game like "Two Truths and a Lie," where you guess which statements are true and which are false.

Example: Story Collaboration

You can start a story, and ChatGPT will continue it.

You: *Let's write a story together! I'll start: "Once upon a time, there was a small village at the foot of a great mountain..."*

ChatGPT: *"...where the villagers believed a dragon lived in a cave at the peak. One day, a young boy decided to climb the mountain and see for himself..."*

This collaborative storytelling allows you to flex your creative muscles while seeing where ChatGPT's imagination takes the story!

Conclusion: Fun and Games with ChatGPT

Using ChatGPT for fun and games opens up endless possibilities for engaging entertainment. Whether you're playing word games, challenging yourself with trivia, or solving personalized puzzles, ChatGPT can be your playful companion. It's not just about fun—it's about keeping your mind sharp, reducing stress, and adding a little excitement to your day.

Incorporating these activities into your routine is a great way to bring joy and mental stimulation into your life. So go ahead—ask ChatGPT to play a game or challenge you with a puzzle. You might just be surprised at how much fun you'll have!

Conclusion:
Your New Adventure with ChatGPT

Congratulations! You've just completed a beginner's guide to ChatGPT, and now you're equipped with a fantastic tool that can make your daily life easier, more organized, and even more fun. Whether you're using it to manage your day, explore new hobbies, or just have some lighthearted fun, ChatGPT is a powerful and friendly companion you can count on.

Let's take a moment to recap what you've learned and how ChatGPT can enrich your life in so many ways:

Staying Organized and Reducing Stress

One of the biggest benefits of using ChatGPT is its ability to help you stay organized. From creating daily to-do lists to helping you break down complex tasks into manageable steps, ChatGPT is there to guide you. With its support, you can approach each day with more clarity and control, reducing the stress that often comes from feeling overwhelmed.

Having Fun with Games and Puzzles

Who says technology is all serious? ChatGPT offers plenty of ways to bring fun into your life. Whether you enjoy word games, trivia, or personalized puzzles, ChatGPT has something for everyone. You can challenge yourself with mental exercises, play creative writing games, or just enjoy a relaxing round of trivia—either on your own or with friends and family.

Learning and Expanding Your Knowledge

ChatGPT is a wealth of knowledge at your fingertips. Anytime you have a question, from historical facts to cooking tips, ChatGPT can provide quick and easy-to-understand answers. It's like having a personal tutor available 24/7! Whether you want to dive deeper into a hobby, pick up a new skill, or simply satisfy your curiosity, ChatGPT makes learning effortless and enjoyable.

Enhancing Communication and Social Connection

Feeling connected is important, and ChatGPT can help you stay in touch with loved ones or make your conversations even more meaningful. Whether you need help composing an email, practicing for a video call, or even coming up with conversation starters, ChatGPT has your back. It's like having a little assistant that can help you express yourself better and stay engaged with the people who matter most.

Exploring Creativity and Personal Interests

ChatGPT isn't just for practical tasks—it's also great for exploring your creative side. You can ask it to help you write a poem, brainstorm ideas for a new hobby, or even create a custom story together. Whether you're rekindling an old passion or discovering a new one, ChatGPT can help you unleash your imagination and dive deeper into the things you love.

Your Partner in Everyday Life

From solving daily challenges to providing entertainment and knowledge, ChatGPT is your go-to companion. It's designed to be easy to use, adaptable, and always ready to help. As you continue exploring all the ways it can assist you, remember that there are no limits to how you can use ChatGPT in your everyday life. The more you engage with it, the more you'll discover.

Now that you've completed this guide, it's time to put what you've learned into practice. Whether you need help managing tasks, having some fun, or exploring new interests, ChatGPT is here to make your life a little easier, a lot more fun, and endlessly more interesting. Happy chatting, and welcome to the exciting world of ChatGPT!

This conclusion wraps up the guide in a way that both summarizes the key points and leaves the reader feeling empowered to continue exploring ChatGPT's capabilities.

Disclaimer

Parts of this ebook were created with the assistance of artificial intelligence (AI) tools, including ChatGPT, to generate and refine content. While every effort has been made to ensure accuracy and clarity, readers should note that AI-generated content may not always reflect the expertise of a human professional. The information presented is for general informational purposes and may not be fully comprehensive or tailored to individual circumstances. For specific advice or concerns, please consult a qualified expert.

This disclaimer highlights the role of AI in the content creation process while encouraging readers to seek expert guidance when needed

Also by Shane Lifeman

Live Free Live Life
We are Jeff and Doris and We Survived Winning The Lottery
Starting Over With Nothings A Rags To Riches Strategy
My Life As A Millionaire Was To Much Work - Living Free Living Life Is Better
From Dream To Reality - A Step By Step Guide How To Move Abroad and Thrive

Standalone
The Power of One Content Repurposing Blueprint - Create Multiple Passive Income Streams
ChatGPT Unlocked - A Beginners Guide For People 50+

Watch for more at www.livefreelivelife.com.

www.ingramcontent.com/pod-product-compliance
Lightning Source LLC
Chambersburg PA
CBHW020625160726
47991CB00002BA/939